M000105259

MANSA'S
Little REMINDERS

Written by A.D. Williams & Kendal Fordham

Illustrated by Taylor Bou

Copyright © 2020 A.D. Williams & Kendal Fordham

Text and illustrations copyright © 2020

All rights reserved.

This is a work of fiction. All names, places, or incidents are the products of the author's imagination or are used fictitiously, and any resemblance to actual persons, living or dead, events, or locales is entirely coincidental. No part of this publication may be reproduced or transmitted in any form or by any means, electronic or mechanical, including photocopying, recording, or by any information storage and retrieval system, now known or to be invented, without permission in writing from the publisher.

For information regarding permissions, contact the publisher at:
www.MansasLittleReminders.com

Author: A.D. Williams and Kendal Fordham Illustrator: Taylor Bou

ISBN: 978-1-7361689-0-5

Published in the United States of America
Printed in the United States of America

DEDICATED TO

A.D. Williams

AUTHOR

My mother: *Reminiscing on the times when it was just you and I.*
We didn't have much, but at the time I couldn't tell.
Your love and work ethic are what fill my memories
and inspire me every day.

Kendal Fordham

AUTHOR

My daughter: *The inspiration I never knew I needed.*

CONTENTS

PRELUDE

Scratching the surface of financial literacy through the reminders of a talking squirrel.

It's amazing what we can accomplish with a little education, inspiration, and support.

Just ask Mark

INTRO

Mark woke up to the sun glaring down on him. The beams of light pierced through the window, shining over his bed. He kept his eyes closed, hoping a cloud would float by. No cloud came. In defeat, he pulled the covers over his head even though he knew sleep would not come back to him. Under his blanket, he lay in darkness, his body still tired but his mind wide-awake...

SCHOOL DAYS: DAY DREAM

Mark was what you would call a daydreamer. He was OK with this, but it always seemed to make everyone else uncomfortable.

Mark's fourth grade teacher, Ms. Langston, was his favorite. She was special. She took time after class to help Mark when he didn't understand her lesson, which saved him the humiliation of raising his hand during class. She never once made him feel dumb.

She did not wear a cape, but to Mark she was a superhero.

Don't get it twisted, she had a tough side too. She once told him he had an overactive imagination after he got caught daydreaming during class. On this particular day, she had to call Mark's name three times before he heard her. When he finally snapped out of it, he could hear some of his classmates snickering behind him. He didn't like the way that felt.

Without thinking, he blurted out the first thing that popped in his head, "If you could see what I'm thinking, you would have nothin' to say. You're just mad your imagination stinks!"

The class erupted with laughter. Ms. Langston slapped a ruler on the table so hard it cracked, scaring the room into an awkward quiet. Mark may get lost in his thoughts sometimes, but he was a good student and far from a class clown. He was smart, did his work on time, and always went out of his way to show Ms. Langston he was trying. He didn't want her to think she was investing her time and energy in him for nothing. Mark didn't want to, but he made himself look at Ms. Langston. It was a quick glance, but that's all it took for him to see the hurt on her beet-red face. That was the first and last time he got sent to the principal's office.

1

We Don't Have Both Money

Mark didn't have a curtain on his window, and he hated it. The sun always woke him up before he was ready. "I'll see if my mom will buy me one next time she's at the discount store," he thought as he hurled himself out of bed and onto his feet. He yawned dramatically, making a noise not unlike a baby dinosaur. As he stood, hands on his hips, scanning the room for yesterday's clothes, a shadow on his windowsill caught his eye.

Sure enough, there sat a small squirrel no bigger than a football. The creature was a creamy brown color, with a beige spot on his chest. Mark couldn't help but think the curious rodent had something on his mind. Something more than just trees and acorns. Mark suddenly felt anxious, realizing it may not be natural to have a stare-off with a squirrel for this long. "What a weird, pointless animal," he said nervously.

Mark picked up his Black Panther T-shirt from yesterday and threw it at the window. The squirrel didn't move, but the look on its face changed. Was it... Could it be... laughing at him? The feeling he got when his classmates snickered at him returned. "Get out of here," Mark grumbled, yet the little rodent stood still. "He must have rabies or something," Mark told himself as he bolted out of the room, leaving the peculiar creature behind.

Mark was running fast as lightning.

"Boy, if you don't slow down!" his mom yelled down the hall.

Despite his grumbling stomach, Mark slowed his roll just in time to sit at the kitchen table. Before he said a word, he began to guzzle down the carton of lemonade that stood half full beside him. Mark loved him some lemonade.

"So help me, Mark, if you don't put that down until you eat!" his mom growled from the kitchen sink. "Do you want bacon or sausage with your eggs," said his Mom.

"Both!" Mark exclaimed.

His mom stared down at him with a familiar look.

"Here we go again," Mark thought to himself. Mark's mom was infamous for her lectures, and she never let an opportunity to give one pass her by.

She let out a long, dramatic sigh—as if to rev the engine of her motherly wisdom. "Look at me, Mark."

Mark turned and looked at his mother's nose. It was easier than looking her in the eyes, and she couldn't tell the difference. They both win this way.

"We don't have both money, and you need to understand what that means."

The only thing keeping Mark from rolling his eyes was the certainty of his mother's open hand smacking him right after. He kept his mouth shut and his eyes still.

"One day, you'll have to do something that people want to get money to buy food for your family. Maybe then you'll understand the value of a dollar."

"All I asked for was sausage and bacon I don't get—"

His mother raised a finger to let him know she wasn't finished talking. "For example, people like playing games on their phone, and they like to use clean toilets, so guess what? Some people get paid to build apps, and other people get paid to clean toilets."

Mark cocked his head in curiosity. "But in most cases, people who clean toilets don't get paid near as much as people who create cool apps!"

When Mark's mom smiled, he knew he had said exactly what she wanted him to. "That's because people like to be entertained more than they care about a clean toilet seat. The more valuable your work is to people, the more you will get paid to do it."

Mark let that sink in and then pointed at the sausage. He waited in silence while his mom finished preparing breakfast.

"You know, what she just said made a lot of sense," said a voice in Mark's head.

Mark stared at his mom as she pranced around the kitchen. The same sunshine that Mark cursed from his bed shined bright on her dark brown skin. The way it reflected off her arms and face made it seem like she was glowing. Like an angel. She was a beautiful woman, and not only Mark thought so. He saw the way people looked at her when they went out in public. Some people would even come up and compliment her. One time while she was at work, one of her customers even asked her on a date!

For as long as he could remember, his mom has worked at the bakery around the corner. She opened the store, she baked the cakes, and she cleaned the bathrooms. She knew how much money the store made and what it took to run it. Mark understood she didn't own the bakery, but he thought she walked and talked like she did. Mark's mom didn't finish college, but you could never tell from talking to her. She had a different type of intelligence, the type you can't learn from books.

Although he had heard his mom talk about money many times before, this conversation was different, and he knew it was not over.

She finished cooking and walked over to Mark. "Mark," she said as she grabbed both his hands gently. "I need you to understand that money doesn't grow on trees." She grabbed a pack of bacon and a box of sausage and walked over to Mark. She laid both in front of him, exposing the price sticker on each. "This bacon costs $4.00, and this sausage costs $3.50."

When Mark thought of money, his second thought was how he wanted to spend it. Usually when he got his hands on a couple bills, his next errand involved the corner store, where he blew it all on something sweet. His unhealthy snacks of choice? Chocolate candy bars and rap snacks.

Mark's mom physically grabbed his attention again by grabbing his face and bringing it to meet hers. "Focus, Mark. Tell me what is $4 plus $3.50?"

"$8.00..." said Mark, a hint of uncertainty in his voice.

"It's $7.50, baby." She paused. "Unless you were including sales tax, then yes, about $8.00."

"Yea, I was," Mark lied. He just couldn't do math that fast. It was his weakest subject. He tried, though, and he owed that to Ms. Langston.

"Good job! But we're not done with our calculation, so hang in there."

Mark had to put maximum effort into preventing an eye roll when she said that. "There are about 30 days in the month. $8.00 times 30 days equals $240.00. Is $240 a lot of money to be spending on JUST sausage and bacon so you can eat it every day?"

"Yes, Mom, I get it now," murmured Mark.

"Whether it's electricity, toys, gas, or something that seems small like bacon and sausage, people like us, who only have one job, need to be smart with their money. And unless you want to be some bum on the side of the road, you need to learn how to do that."

Mark was lost in his thoughts when his mother placed the paper plate in front of him. Although his mom's speech took a million minutes longer than it should have, he understood why he couldn't have bacon and sausage. He also understood he wanted his family to have as much bacon and sausage as their heart desired. There was so much he still had to learn, but he promised himself right there, at the kitchen table, that no matter what, he wouldn't give up. He would learn to be so smart with money that he would provide a life for himself and his loved ones that even his mother couldn't understand. Mark shook his head in confirmation of his own thoughts.

Then he ate like he had never had breakfast before.

2

Acorns

The sun was hiding behind a big cloud as he walked toward the backyard. Where was that dumb cloud this morning when he wanted to go back to sleep?

Mark loved throwing acorns into the open lot behind his house. It was impossible for him to run out of ammunition. The acorns fell from a huge oak tree. One so big that he always imagined having a treehouse built in it.

He picked up the biggest nut he could find and focused on a target 10 feet away. He had discovered, if he closed his eyes and imagined himself hitting his mark, he had a much better chance of nailing it when he threw it in real life. Once he conquered one object, he would move on to another farther away. It was a game that he made up when he had no one else to hang out with, which was a lot.

He couldn't have been playing more than five minutes when an acorn dropped out of the tree and hit Mark smack on the head. "Ouch!" he screamed. Mark spent hours in that same spot every weekend, but never had an acorn hit him in the head that hard. In fact, it felt like it was thrown. Mark looked up and marveled at the sheer size of the tree's branches. He quickly concluded he could never pinpoint where the nut fell from, so he moved on to his next target.

As the wind blew and the birds chirped, Mark grabbed a handful of acorns and took aim at an empty trash can about twenty feet away. It was rusted and half-buried in leaves. The old can had been there for as long as he could remember, and today, it was his second target. He narrowed in on the dirty old can and whispered, "I'm going to hit that trash can right in the center."

He paused, keeping his eyes fixed ahead, and repeated himself loudly, "I'm going to hit that trash can right in the center!" He closed his eyes and imagined himself throwing the nut as hard as he could. In his vision, he could hear the loud tink of the acorn hitting the rusty tin with so much force it put a dent in it. It was right there in his mind. He could see it. All he had to do was bring it to life. He opened his eyes slowly. Everything around him was frozen in time. He took one giant step forward and pulled his arm back as far as he possibly could, like a human slingshot, when out of nowhere a high-pitched voice shouted behind him.

"You should really find your own acorns to throw."

Mark turned around so quickly he lost his balance and fell flat on his butt. He frantically searched his surroundings, his heart beating out of his chest. He started listing off normal things around him to calm himself down. There were leaves, lots of leaves. The tree, of course. Candy wrappers and soda cans. A shopping cart. And then a squirrel.

Mark stood up nervously. "Is that?... No that can't be..." he said out loud. "Squirrels don't talk."

The squirrel was closer and stared back at Mark with the same attitude it had when it sat on his windowsill. "Well, this one does. I'm serious, have you thought about finding your own acorns?" the squirrel repeated.

Mark's uncle once told him dogs can smell fear, but people can only tell if you are scared by how you act. He told Mark that, if he ever felt scared and weak, to pretend like he was confident and strong. "Never let anyone know you're scared. Fake it until you make it, nephew," he would say. His uncle had failed to mention anything about how to act around talking squirrels, so he wasn't sure how to handle this specific situation. Go figure.

The squirrel started tapping his paw against the ground, clearly demonstrating his impatience.

Mark decided to pretend like he wasn't scared, despite his mouth being so dry he thought he might swallow his tongue. "No, I have never thought about that... I don't like to eat acorns like I assume you do. I only like throwing them."

The squirrel rolled its eyes dramatically. "Well, guess what? I love them. And each time you play with them, you throw away something that I value. These acorns give me a reason to wake up every morning. When I am having a bad day, they keep me motivated and happy. Not only that, they taste great!"

Mark didn't have a response, but he also didn't have enough control over his legs to run home, so he just stood there awkwardly.

"I eat some of these acorns, and what I don't eat, I bury and save for another time. This is how I make sure I never run out."

The squirrel's comments reminded Mark of the bacon and sausage conversation from earlier.

"What do you value?" demanded the squirrel.

"Money." Mark didn't have to think hard about that one.

The squirrel nodded. "That is a good place to start, but money is only one part. I love acorns, not just because they are valuable, but also because they bring me great happiness. Because acorns bring me joy, I am always motivated to go get more, even when they are harder to find."

Mark was lost, and somehow, the squirrel must have noticed.

"Money alone will not bring you happiness, my friend, rather it's what you do to make money that should bring you joy. This way, when things get hard, you will still be motivated to continue to make money. Because you love what you do!"

Whether or not this squirrel was real, he was making a lot of sense.

"If you like money, you should think about how to find it, how to take care of it, and not waste it like you do with my acorns. Life is a lot sweeter if you can find your acorns!"

And with that, the squirrel scurried up the tree and disappeared into the web of branches in the sky.

3

The Lemonade Stand

Mark woke up at dusk feeling heavy and confused. He had spent so much time outside in the sun that he must have fallen asleep right when he got home. As groggy as he felt, there was no way he could go to bed after napping so late in the day. His mom would certainly be upset with him. On the bright side, his squirrel friend was nowhere in sight, and the thought of this made him relax a little.

Mark quietly made his way to the small front room where the TV was located. He didn't want to disturb his mom as she lay in bed watching her show. If Mark could keep quiet, he knew she would stay there the rest of the night. Mark put on socks so his feet wouldn't make any sound as he shuffled and slid along the laminate floor. When he made it to the front room, he quietly sat on the side of the couch closest to the TV. That side of the couch had springs that didn't creak. No noise is good noise. Just as Mark pressed the power button on the remote, he heard his mom pause her show. "Jeez, I just can't catch a break today," Mark thought.

"Mark? You in that front room?"

Mark didn't respond.

A long, silent pause followed before his mother dramatically exhaled in frustration. "Go take a shower and get ready for bed! Tomorrow is Sunday, and we have to go the store."

Thankful she hadn't noticed his long nap, Mark shrugged off his failed attempt to watch TV and headed toward the bathroom they shared. He took a shower, granted a fast one.

The thought of closing his eyes seemed like torture, so Mark opted to stare at the ceiling instead. The conversation he had under the tree was playing on repeat in his mind. He couldn't press pause or change the channel like he could with the TV remote, but he supposed this was better than nothing.

Values... money... save... The squirrel's comments bounced off the walls of his head so fast it made him dizzy—but the fun kind of dizzy, like when you get off a roller-coaster for the second time.

Mark awoke the next morning excited to start the day. Not even the rays of sun beaming through his window could bring him down. When he got on his feet, he walked over to the window with outstretched arms and yawned away the remnants of sleep. There was no squirrel on the windowsill today, and that was just fine with Mark. Today was a shopping day, and—if his mom was in a good mood—Mark would be allowed to pick out his favorite food and a toy.

The aisles and aisles of stocked shelves packed full of colorful labels and shiny newness gave Mark goose bumps. He often fantasized about sneaking into the bathroom of the store during regular business hours and staying there until after they closed. Once the store manager locked the door, he would triumphantly emerge from the bathroom and walk down each aisle. He could then read and touch all the different toys and food without anyone rushing him. A boy could dream, right?

He wanted to be at the door, ready to go, so his mom wouldn't have to wait on him. For this to work in his favor, she had to be in a good mood, and Mark's mom liked to get to the store as soon as it opened. There would be fewer people there, and she could use all her coupons without holding up the line.

Her car was in the shop, so they walked to the city bus stop about a half mile down the road. Mark was low-key happy they had to take public transportation. He hated his Mom's car. It was old and rusted on the top, the passenger side door always got jammed, and the air only worked when it wanted to. Earlier in the school year, he told his mom he wanted to start riding the bus to school because he had made friends with some classmates who lived in a neighborhood close by. It was a big fat lie. The truth was he was embarrassed by how poor that ugly car made him look when she dropped him off. A lot of the boys Mark tried to hang out with at school got dropped off in newer cars with big screens in the center consoles and TVs in the head rests. One kid even Ubered sometimes.

He felt bad about lying to his mom, but it was better than making her feel bad. Nonetheless, it confused him why they struggled with money even when his mom worked so much. Maybe instead of working harder, his mom could work smarter, but what did that really mean? I bet that dumb little squirrel would know the answer.

As soon as the sliding doors parted, a bell went beep beep, and a gust of ice-cold air hit Mark's face. He closed his eyes and smiled. "That has to be what it feels like when you walk through the gates of heaven," Mark said.

His mom chuckled—a good sign that he may get to buy something. His eyes began to wander.

Mark's mom went straight to the grocery section. Mark took a moment to watch his mother shop. She picked up steaks and chicken and compared the prices. She picked up two different milks to see which one seemed bigger. She checked her coupons to make sure none of her items had cheaper options on sale. As Mark's mom filled up the shopping cart, his mind began to shift.

"Find your own acorns," he whispered to himself.

"What was that, baby?" Mark's mom said as she reached for bananas.

Mark couldn't believe what he was about to say, but he knew if he didn't try, he would always wonder what would have happened if he did. "Mom, do you know how to make lemonade?"

Mark's mom raised one eyebrow in curiosity. "Yes. Why do you ask?"

Mark thought about the squirrel and everything he said. In truth, Mark hadn't really stopped thinking about what the squirrel said since he said it. "Um, well, I really love lemonade, and I think I want to learn how to make some so I can sell it to people. That way I can buy my own games and stuff. I don't know, maybe if I make enough, I can help you out, too."

Mark's mom's jaw about fell off her face. "That is a great idea! But before we buy all the ingredients, we need a plan." She motioned for Mark to follow her to the far wall of the store, where a long blue metal bench sat. She sat down and patted the spot next to her. "Do you know what a business plan is?"

Mark thought it seemed pretty straightforward. "A plan that describes my business!?"

"Exactly. A business plan will be able to tell another person exactly *how* you plan on selling lemonade, *when* you plan on selling it, *where* you will conduct your business, and *why*."

The Business Plan

She pulled out her phone, opened the notes app, and titled her entry, *Mark's Business Plan*.

"What do you want to sell?" she said to Mark.

"The best lemonade on the Southside," said Mark.

Mark's mom gave him a side-eyed glare. "Watch your mouth."

Mark held back a toothy grin. He couldn't help it. He was vibrating with excitement! He fixed his face before responding, "Yes, ma'am."

"Who do you want to sell lemonade to?" she continued.

Mark thought about this. Doesn't everyone love lemonade? I suppose not everyone loves it as much as I do, but certainly no one has ever tasted an ice cold glass of lemonade on a hot day and spat it out. "Everyone?" Mark said.

Mark's mom shook her head. "It's better to be specific. When you have a clear idea of who you're selling to, you have a better chance of being successful because you can focus on only those people. Once you've successfully sold to that group, THEN you can go bigger and sell to more people."

Mark's eyes widened. It was just like the game he invented with the acorns and the targets. Mark couldn't help but feel like all of this—the game, the acorns, the squirrel—were all connected.

"What will the cost be for a cup of the best lemonade on the Southside?" she said with a smile. She was proud of her son and wanted him to be successful at everything he did. She knew he had what it took to be great because she did too. This could be the beginning of something big for him, she thought. As she watched Mark desperately try to hide his excitement, she admitted to herself that she was excited too. She waited patiently for her baby boy to respond.

Mark furrowed his brow. "I'm not sure, Mom. I don't want to make it so cheap that I don't make any money, but I also don't want to make it so expensive no one wants to buy any."

This was a tricky one. He knew the solution would involve math, and without paper and a calculator, Mark felt discouraged. Mark's mother was no stranger to his struggle with the subject. She had paid just about every teenager within a five-mile radius of their house to tutor him.

When he felt his mom's hand rub his shoulder, he had to fight back the lump forming in his throat. Maybe this wasn't a good idea. Maybe I'm not smart enough for this, Mark thought.

"Baby, there was a time when someone had to teach the smartest man in the world how to tie his shoes." She paused. "How can you know something if someone doesn't teach you first?"

Mark nodded, his head still looking at the ground. Maybe it wasn't too late to just get some candy and call it a day.

"We'll talk about this one after we make our lemonade, sound OK?"

Mark nodded, thankful she chose to move on to something else.

"Where do you want to sell the lemonade?"

Mark didn't have to think long. "The town park! A lot of people will be out there now that the weather is heatin' up."

"And why do you think people will buy your lemonade?"

"Because it's going to be hot and I'm going to put the stand right where the trail and the playground cross, so people running or walking their dogs and kids who are on the swings or jungle gym can see what I'm selling." Mark smiled. He could tell his mom was surprised by how much thought he had put into this already.

Now it was Mark's mom who had the lump in her throat. She hugged Mark and whispered in his ear, "This is the start of so many great things for you."

4

Cuzzo and the Candy Store

Mark could feel the sweat zigzagging down his back as they walked in the front door. His mother had squeezed all she could into her grocery buggy, but everything that didn't fit Mark had to carry. The long journey home left Mark exhausted.

"I could use a glass of the best lemonade in Southside right about now," his mom said as he turned to walk down the hall to his room.

Mark acknowledged her sarcasm with a fake chuckle out of respect. As he opened the door to his bedroom, he heard his mother's warning.

"Don't sleep for long. Your cousin will be here in two hours, and you need to shower. You smell like a wet dog."

As he shut his door, he could hear his mom laughing at her own insult. If he wasn't so tired, he would reply with something slick to take advantage of her playful mood.

As his bedroom door shut, Mark peeled off his sweaty T-shirt, throwing it in the general vicinity of his dirty clothes hamper. What was the point of that thing, anyway? His dirty clothes lay sprawled around the empty bin but rarely in it. He spun around and collapsed faceup on his mattress. He knew his mom would insist he take a shower before getting in his bed, but the ceiling fan was more convincing. The metal blades blew gusts of air that chilled his bare skin, still moist with sweat. Mark welcomed the goose bumps emerging on his arms. He has always preferred the sensation of being cold rather than hot.

Cuzzo was a couple years older than Mark, but she was by far his favorite out of all twenty-two cousins. His favoritism was partially due to her dad, Uncle Craig. Uncle Craig had his own business and was known in the family as Mom's "smart" brother. He would never call him daddy, but Uncle Craig was about as close to a father as Mark was going to get. He was nothing short of awesome in Mark's eyes.

As he lingered somewhere between sleep and consciousness, Mark reminisced on the many walks he and Cuzzo had shared over the years. Many of those walks led right to the corner store where Mark and Cuzzo would spend the $5 Uncle Craig gave them whenever he visited. Yet another reason to be excited for her weekend stays.

Mark remembered one particular trip because it was the first time Cuzzo made him feel stupid. It happened more often than Mark liked to admit because Cuzzo was smart. When she wasn't watching her daddy run his business, she was helping him.

He remembered this weekend was hot. He and Cuzzo had walked slowly to the store, making small talk about school and sports. Time went by slowly as the sun beat down on their backs, but eventually Mark could make out the corner stone amid the dust and heat waves reflecting off the road.

When Mark flung open the store door, a familiar beep beep announced their entry to Mr. Lee, the store clerk. He lowered the newspaper and acknowledged their presence with a narrow-eyed stare that said, "You touch it you buy it."

Cuzzo ignored Mr. Lee's unwelcoming attitude, and Mark didn't even notice it. The door hadn't even shut before Mark was walking up to the register with two king size candy bars.

Cuzzo shook her head and laughed.

"What?! I'm a man who knows what he wants," he joked. As he waited in line, Mark flipped the candy bars over in his hand. He noticed the price had gone up 50 cents to $2.50 a bar, and after sales tax, Mr. Lee was happy to let Mark know he was 35 cents short.

Lucky for Mark, the silver-haired lady waiting impatiently behind him forked up the extra change. Her random act of kindness was more intended to get Mark out of her way. As Mark exited the corner store, he heard her ask Mr. Lee for a carton of cigarettes.

Cuzzo always took her time, so Mark opted to eat his chocolate outside on the curb. Mark was halfway done with his second candy bar when Cuzzo finally emerged. She was a lengthy chick, with long awkward legs and braces. She used to get picked on for those legs until she started playing sports. Cuzzo was a way better athlete than Mark. But Mark's mom assured him one day he'd hit a growth spurt and be more of a competitor. He was still waiting for that growth spurt.

As they moseyed back home, Mark noticed Cuzzo's plastic bag clinked and clanked with every step. Mark stared at her, confused.

"Boy, what are you staring at?" she asked.

"You have at least $3 left in that bag. You could have bought something else." "Because I want to save my $3. Any time I get money from anything, I save half of it. I've been doing it since I was ten years old."

Mark was surprised. "You're not worried someone's going to take all that cash?"

Cuzzo laughed a little. "Boy, you really don't know what you don't know, do ya?" This is where Mark felt dumb.

Out of pity, or maybe guilt, Cuzzo explained. "My daddy opened me up a bank account when I was real little. He started giving me $20 every two weeks if I did my chores and helped out at his shop. Each time he handed me the $20 bill, he said the same thing, 'Bosses pay themselves first.' If I ignored him and went and spent my money on candy or toys, he wouldn't say nothing. I just wouldn't get my $20 the next go around—even if I did everything I was supposed to. I learned real quick how to manage my money."

Mark heard the doorbell ring through his slumber. The modest first ring was followed by three more in quick succession.

DingDongDingDongDingDong.

"Mark, your cousin is here. I hope you cleaned up! Now get that door before she break my bell!" screamed Mom.

"Yes, ma'am!" said Mark as he ran to the door to let her in.

A big toothy smile greeted him as he opened the door. "What's good!"

"My nap was pretty great until you woke me up," he joked.

19

"Sleep is for the weak," she replied playfully.

"I was just thinking about one of our candy-store adventures before you barged in. Do you want to go outside before it gets dark?"

Mark's mom kindly reminded them to be in before dark or there would be hell to pay, but they were both already halfway down the driveway.

5

The Nice Hood

When Cuzzo came to visit, Mark's mom gave him a little more freedom. He and Cuzzo usually made a point to visit the rich neighborhoods about nine blocks down the street from his. They had an hour and a half before dusk, so they started toward the gated communities that surrounded the neighborhoods they wanted to see. Mark knew a couple kids from school who stayed there, but he never got invited over to hang out. They weren't close like that.

The big iron gates were usually open around this time, allowing him and Cuzzo to walk right through like they lived there.

Uncle Craig had told them long ago, when they walked through neighborhoods like this, they needed to remember three things. "Keep your hands out of your pockets at all times, smile and wave at everybody who walks by, and always stay on the sidewalk."

Mark still didn't understand why he made such a big deal out of this, but he would never dare argue with Uncle Craig.

As they entered the first gate, the smell of fresh-cut grass danced on their noses. The tall columns, perfect landscaping, and shiny cars that rested in driveways were fuel to Mark's imagination. As they walked, he collected the picture-perfect mental images like prized treasure. He could see it now: his mom tending to the rose bushes outside as he pulled up in his flashy convertible after school.

"The good life..." Mark said under his breath.

Cuzzo thumped him upside the head. "Boy, what are you doing?!"

Cuzzo was familiar with Mark's strange tendency to drift off. She didn't make him feel bad about it though, which he appreciated more than she knew.

"Can we go back and shoot some hoops before dark?" asked Cuzzo.

"Yea, I'm cool with that," Mark answered, trying to hide the disappointment in his voice. He wanted to see more.

As they walked back through the winding brick roads of the upper-class neighborhood, Mark noticed a familiar car speeding down the road. The car looked more like a small spaceship than a vehicle, even sounded like one too. Not that Mark had seen many spaceships in his eleven years of life, but it couldn't be that far off.

The bright yellow spaceship turned into the driveway two houses in front of their path. The purr of the engine went kaput, and out climbed Mr. Stewart. His brown hair all shiny and slick. The way he walked in his tailored blue suit and pink tie made him look silly and important at the same time.

Mark recognized the car because it sometimes picked his classmate Jimmy Stewart up from school. Jimmy was the kind of kid you wanted to be friends with. He lived in a huge house, was good at sports, all the girls had crushes on him, he was super smart, he stood up against bullies, and if you were in his inner circle you got to go on vacations with his family to places like Spain or whatever. Mark didn't want Jimmy to see him right now. He didn't know how to explain why he was walking down his street without sounding stupid.

Jimmy was once Mark's assigned partner for a science project on the solar system. As a result, Mark was invited over a few afternoons so they could fine-tune the project. It had to be perfect. When they needed a break, they would go outside and throw the football around. To Mark's dismay, no REAL friendship blossomed out of their project dates.

Mark sometimes wondered if it was because of the three thousand questions he asked.

"Why are you gone on the weekends so much?"

"My dad's gone a lot for work, so we don't see him a lot during the week. To make up for it, my mom plans weekend trips so we can 'bond' or whatever," Jimmy answered.

"Well what does your Dad do?"

"He's an engineer. He helps companies build cool things like apps, computers, and robots. My mom does the payroll for the company—basically she makes sure all the employees get their paychecks."

Mark realized he had no idea what an engineer did. He'd have to google that later. "Oh that's cool. So your parents must really like each other if they are able to spend so much time together."

"I mean, they fight sometimes about dumb stuff, but they also hold hands and kiss too, so I guess so."

Jimmy paused for a moment before he threw the football back at Mark. "Are your parents divorced? I never see your dad come to any school stuff."

Mark's stomach lurched. There was no way he was about to tell the coolest kid in school that not only had he never met his dad, he had never even seen a picture of him. He could walk by Mark right now, and he wouldn't know the difference between him and a stranger.

When Mark was younger, he was obsessed with the idea of finding his dad. Every time he saw a man about his mom's age, he would look at him closely, looking for the slightest resemblance. "Maybe that's him," he would say to himself.

"Yea, they got divorced when I was little, and he moved really far away for work. Like out of the country. I go and visit him once a year," Mark lied through his teeth.

"Ah, dude, I'm sorry. That must really stink. I don't know what I would do if my dad wasn't around. He teaches me so much stuff."

Mark could feel that lump forming in his throat again. "Get it together, Mark," he scolded himself. "You ain't no baby, and you ain't weak. You don't need a daddy. You'll make it on your own, and it will feel twice as good."

Mark took the opportunity to change the subject. "So where did you guys go for spring break this year?"

"Fiji. Super long plane ride, but the seats were like beds, and we each had our own TV with every movie you could think of, so it wasn't too bad. The steak could have been better."

Mark hung on his response for a second. "Fiji... like the fancy water in the gas station?"

Jimmy laughed loudly. "Yea, dude, like the water in the gas station. Speaking of which, my mom always keeps some chilled in the fridge, you want one?"

As they walked toward the kitchen, Mark admired the pictures hanging on the wall, each acting as a window into the adventures of Jimmy's family. There were beaches, sunsets, Jimmy riding a camel's backs, even one with Jimmy's little sister getting kissed by a dolphin! Mark had never even been to the beach much less been kissed by a giant sea mammal.

"So what do you do for fun here in our boring old town when you're not traveling around the world like a famous person?" Mark asked sarcastically.

Jimmy laughed. "Well, grades are really important to my folks, so I try to do my homework early before my mom makes dinner, and if I don't have practice for basketball or football, I read and maybe play some video games before I pass out."

Mark was satisfied with this answer. At least they had video games in common. Mark couldn't remember the last time he read a book when he didn't have to. Maybe he should start doing that. It's obviously working for Jimmy.

As they walked through Jimmy's mansion, Mark noticed how incredibly organized and clean it was. Everything had its own place. The walls were all chalk white, blue, and yellow, making the rooms seem even bigger and brighter. The same was to be said of Jimmy's room. The bed was made and pillows fluffed. All of his furniture matched, and no dirty clothes covered the floor. The only slight mess, if you could even call it that, was a big pile of technology and finance magazines that sat on his desk. "Is this what you meant by reading? Why would you wanna read technology magazines?" Mark asked.

"I hear my dad always talking about this kind of stuff on his business calls, and he gets these in the mail every month. After he reads them, he gives them to me to read. When I'm done, we quiz each other about what we learned."

"Your dad doesn't go to work at an office?"

"Nope," said Jimmy. "He works for himself, so he can work from wherever he wants. Sometimes he works from our other house downtown."

Mark assumed everybody went to work like his mom, at the same time every week, at the same place. He also never considered people could have more than one house. "I want to work for myself too," Mark thought to himself.

His cousin looked at him like he was crazy. "Boy, you have been sitting there staring at them people's house for ten minutes. Are you OK?"

"Yea, I'm cool. I am just thinking... thinking about my acorns and my lemonade stand."

Cuzzo almost coughed on her response. "Your what?"

6

Let's Do It Together Then

They made it back to the house before dark, but the walk had made them sticky and smelly. They decided to pass on the basketball idea. Mark was fine with that. Less of an opportunity for Cuzzo to beat his butt at her natural sport.

Once they got inside, Mark focused on a new task, and after asking a hundred different ways, Mark's mom finally agreed to order pizza.

Mark's mom said yes more than no when Cuzzo was in town. She thought Cuzzo was a good influence on him. Mark didn't disagree, but she could be a tad bit bossy. It wasn't her fault, she was just used to being in control, just like her dad. It was because of this he knew his cousin was biting at the bit to hear about his lemonade stand idea. He'd never forget the look on her face when he tried to explain how acorns and his lemonade stand idea were connected.

"You see, squirrels eat a lot of acorns, but they don't just eat everything they find. They bury acorns they don't need right then and save them for later. The question is not if they need acorns. They know they need them to survive. It's how are they going to get them? How are they going to make sure they always have more than they need?"

Cuzzo's face was hard to read. She either didn't care about what he was saying, or she thought he had lost his mind.

Either way, Mark continued, "Right now, all I know is I NEED to make it one day so I can give my mom the life she deserves. So I can travel around the world with my kids. So I don't have to live paycheck to paycheck! I just don't know how to do it. I need to learn how to collect my own acorns. A lot of 'em."

Based on her reaction, he decided against bringing up the talking squirrel.

The doorbell rang just in time to save Mark from the awkward situation that was unfolding.

"The pizza man is here! Grab the money off the counter and tell 'im that he can keep the change," yelled Mom.

Mark slid down the tile hallway in his socks like a rock star and grabbed the money from the kitchen counter. He smelled the crisp green bill. His mom would have yelled at him if she saw, but she was in the other room.

"That's disgusting, Mark. Do you know how many hands have touched that?" she would have barked.

The smell of money was always cool to Mark, and he didn't think it was all that gross anyway. Besides the smell, there was something about holding money and paying for things that Mark had enjoyed since he was small. Whether it was pizza, groceries, or even stamps at the post office. He loved the feeling. It made him feel like an adult.

Mark's butt barely touched the seat before he ripped open the cardboard box. He preferred cheese pizza while the girls loved pepperoni, so they got half and half. Initially, no one spoke. Only the sounds of chewing, swallowing, and happiness could be heard circulating the small wooden kitchen table.

Mark's mom paused as she eyed which piece she wanted next. "I'm glad no one is here watching y'all eat like this. They would ask me if I ever fed y'all before. Both y'all just greedy!" she said, laughing.

Cuzzo and Mark glanced at each other. Mark's mom was eating just as much and just as fast, but they knew better than to bring that to her attention. Mark's mom could dish it, but she sure wasn't good at taking it.

They ate everything but the pizza box. Mark could have eaten that whole pizza on his own, but he didn't have the guts to ask his mom to start buying two pies. The last thing he wanted to hear is another "we don't have two pizza money" speech.

Another plus about eating pizza was the cleanup. No silverware was needed, and the paper plates didn't need to be washed and dried. Now, if Mark's mom had made beanies and weenies, another fan favorite, there would have been a world of plates, silverware, and pots for Mark to scrub after. They had a dishwasher in the kitchen, but Mark was told it ran up the water bill. It was never to be used under any circumstances. If he objected, he was called lazy, among other insulting names. Pizza didn't come with any drama.

The pink rays that cascaded across the sky indicated that daylight was ending. Mark watched as Cuzzo's eyes fluttered as she battled sleep. Mark wasn't tired, and neither was his cousin—she was just bored. Usually around this time, they were busy building forts, making up raps, or playing PlayStation, but not tonight. Things were quiet. So quiet that Mark's mom stopped by the room a few times, asking if they were OK.

He assured his mom they were fine. "We're not babies, Mom."

Mark's mom gave a look that told him his next words needed to be chosen carefully.

Mark decided to not choose any at all and turned back around to face the TV. As Cuzzo slept, Mark let his mind sort through the day's events. By far, his favorite part was walking through the rich neighborhood.

The sudden sound of his cousin's voice scared him upright. Mark didn't even realize he'd dozed off.

"So are you gonna tell me about the lemonade stand because I'm still pretty lost on what the heck that has to do with acorns."

It took Mark several seconds to realize what planet he was on, much less understand what she was talking about. "Well, yesterday I got my mom to buy me the ingredients I need to make the lemonade. We even made a business plan."

His cousin seemed interested.

"I told her that I wanted to sell what we made. That way I can have my own money and start to save it, kinda like squirrels do with acorns." Mark looked at his window, where the talking squirrel once sat. "I want to save money like you do. I want to buy nice things and go on trips like Jimmy. Man, I just want my own acorns like that crazy talking squirrel!"

His cousin cut him off, "What squirrel?"

Get it together, Mark. JEEZ.

"Nothing, I just think that a lemonade stand would be cool to try." "Let's do it together then," said his cousin matter-of-factly.

Mark couldn't fight the smile that spread like wildfire across his face.

"My Dad was telling me how he and his friend started a business together. They opened up shops and sold clothes. He said that if you're going to have a business partner, ya better have a good one 'cus it can make ya or break ya."

The Golden Door

"I know y'all not still sleep in there," yelled Mark's mom.

It was almost noon. After their conversation, they stayed up and planned every detail of the lemonade stand. It wasn't until two in the morning that they decided to go to bed. Mark slept on a makeshift mattress made of old comforters while Cuzzo got to sleep in his bed. It didn't matter at that point in the night, though. They both couldn't keep their eyes open. Mark could have fallen asleep on a bed of nails at that point.

Mark's mom called for Cuzzo to come take a shower and get ready in her room. Her dad was coming to pick her up in a few. "Mark, make sure you get some clean clothes on, too."

Mark's eyes darted around the room for something to wear. He had straightened up, per his mother's request, but in Mark's language, straighten up meant throwing everything under furniture.

Where had he put his Black Panther shirt? Surely, he could get one more day out of it before it smelled too bad. He was so deep in thought that the loud thump thump thump on his window nearly gave him a heart attack. He looked up to find none other than his squirrel buddy. Mark smiled. Over the last couple of days, he had wondered if he would ever see him again.

He ran over to the window and opened it with so much excitement, he almost broke it. "Hey what's your name anyway?" he exclaimed.

"Mansa!" he said through a bucktooth smile. Mansa was in much better spirits than when he had scolded Mark about the acorns.

"That is a strange name. Is that African or something?"

33

"Everything is weird to somebody. It could be African, but it's also mine!"

Mark laughed. "Well, Mansa, my name is Mark, and I gotta say, I'm glad to see you again."

"Have you put any thought into our conversation under the big acorn tree?" asked Mansa.

"Yes! That's why I'm so glad to see you. I have so much to tell you. Because of you I'm FINALLY on to something."

The squirrel leaned in like a proud teacher. Mansa had been watching from a distance far before he ever approached Mark's window that first time. Mark didn't realize this, but any time he was outside or sitting in his room, Mansa wasn't far behind. It took him a while, but eventually Mansa decided to risk it all and talk to Mark.

Today was a proud day for Mansa. He was impressed with the progress Mark had made, both in his actions and his thinking about the future.

"I had an idea about lemonade because I freakin' love lemonade, so my mom helped me make a business plan! Then I kind of got discouraged until I saw Jimmy's dad's car! So yea, my mom's gonna teach me how to make it, and Cuzzo's going to help me because she already knows how to sell stuff, and I'm going to find my own acorns, and it's all because of YOU!"

The squirrel's eyes widened. "Whoa, whoa, slow down there, Mark. I am super excited that you and your cousin are working together. I think she brings value to the team. You hold the keys!"

Mark cocked his head like a puppy that just heard a fire truck for the first time. "The keys to what..."

"The golden door of success."

Mark frowned. "That doesn't seem real. Is this another one of your strange riddles?"

"When people come together with clever ideas and are willing to work, great things can happen, Mark! You could be dirt poor, but once you find your purpose—your acorns—you have the opportunity to walk through the golden door, and that's how you move up to the next level."

Mark felt strange inside. At first, he thought he might be nervous, but no, this felt different than that. It was a new sensation. A mixture of fire and joy. Motivated. That was a better way to describe it. Mark closed his eyes and smiled, taking it all in.

Cuzzo's heavy fists hitting his open door brought Mark back to his senses. "You in here talking to yourself half naked?"

Mark grabbed his Black Panther shirt to cover his bare torso. When he turned back toward the squirrel, he was nowhere in sight.

7

Uncle Craig

Mark was annoyed with Cuzzo for barging in on his conversation with Mansa. His feelings quickly changed when he heard a familiar sound from out front.

BEEEEEEEP BEEEEEEEP

The heavy-centered, broad-shouldered man laid on his car horn, announcing his arrival to the entire neighborhood. In a terrible British accent he shouted, "And here arrives the Duke of Kensington, Sir Craig Robert Williams!" Uncle Craig got out of the car, clapping dramatically at his own show.

Mark's mom shook her head as if she wasn't entertained, but she was. "You're your biggest fan, Craig," she said as she turned to go back inside.

If it were anyone else pulling up in her driveway, Mark knew she would have had a fit, but Uncle Craig could get away with almost anything around here.

Growing up, Mark would hear stories about his uncle at family barbeques and birthdays.

"Your Uncle Craig is something else, boy," his auntie would start saying after a few too many adult drinks. "Known for helping and hurting," she laughed. "Once your uncle started making money doing his small business thing, he was always there for his people. If you needed a dollar, he would give you a dollar," she said matter-of-factly.

She turned and got closer to Mark's face and pointed a long, hot pink fingernail right at his nose.

"But, boy oh boy, you better give him his money back on time."

With that said, she slapped her knee, spilling Mark's fruit punch all over his new khaki shorts. Auntie didn't care, or she didn't notice.

"If you didn't give him his money back, that was it. You never got another dime out of him. You wasn't his friend, his cousin, as a matter of fact, in my case, you weren't his sister no more!" She chuckled as she took another swig of her drink.

Mark assumed that meant she had not paid Uncle Craig his money.

"Craig wouldn't hurt a fly, but he demanded respect, and I gotta say I respect my big brother. He taught me about debt the hard way, and I'm a better woman because of it."

His aunt might be tipsy, but she was making sense. When you take money from somebody, you better pay them back, and you best do it when you say you will. That was a well-known rule in his family, thanks to Uncle Craig.

Mark thought about his lemonade stand. If he borrowed money from his uncle and didn't pay him back, he knew his uncle would take his whole business. Just like Mark's mom was infamous for her long lectures, Uncle Craig was notorious for his real life lessons. Mark wasn't ready to think about that, so when he said bye to Cuzzo and his Uncle Craig he didn't bring up the lemonade stand, and he hoped Cuzzo wouldn't either, at least not yet.

8

More Lemonade

The alarm on Mark's clock was the sound of a rooster cock-a-doodle-doing. Mark had never been around real-life roosters, but based on the noise one made, Mark didn't think he would like them very much.

Today was the day they were going to put Mark's lemonade stand idea into action. Mark rubbed his eyes as he stared at the alarm clock. It took him awhile to figure out how to turn it off. He had never used it. No one had. The thing must be at least ten years old. He could tell by what type of Apple USB port it had. He planned on using it more now that he was trying to build a business. Uncle Craig said most successful people get up early because the most productive time of day is when the rest of the world is still dreaming. Mark decided to give it a try, hence the alarm clock.

The plan was pretty straightforward. They would go down to the town park just before the hottest part of the day and set up the stand and the surprisingly artistic sign they had created. Cuzzo had drawn up a rough sketch of how the lemonade should be displayed on the stand.

But the best part? The lemonade was actually delicious.

Easily the best he had ever had. Rightfully so, they had stayed up half the night prepping so the juice could marinate overnight—apparently a very necessary step. Mark was amazed at the amount of work that went into making the old southern recipe his grandmother gave them. The directions were very detailed. Perfectly numbered and bulleted in his grandmother's neat cursive, a type of writing Mark had never been taught in school.

Mark's mom did most of the slicing of the fruit because she didn't trust Cuzzo or Mark with the sharp blades of her cooking knives. That was probably for the best. Mark was in charge of the mixing and tasting, which he had no issue with at all. It may have been three in the morning by the time they were done, but Mark had drunk so much of the sugary drink he was wide awake.

When they were finally done for the night, they sat at the kitchen table to rest and observe the fruits of their labor. No pun intended.

"Mark, do you know how much you want to sell these for?"

Mark had forgotten they had skipped that part of the business plan as they sat in the grocery store. He hesitantly looked up at his mother who already had a piece of paper and pencil ready. Mark didn't try to hide his dismay. Why would she wait until freakin' three in the morning to do the hardest part?

Mark's mother pulled out the receipt form the grocery store, placing it gingerly in front of Mark and Cuzzo. Mark looked at the piece of crinkled paper, scanning the long list of items. Some line items were his mother's groceries, others the ingredients for his lemonade. His mother handed him the pen and slid over the piece of paper. Mark knew what he had to do. She didn't HAVE to tell him, but she did anyway.

"Add 'em up, boy."

Mark carefully picked out the ingredients and wrote them on the paper. Across from each item, he listed its price. He was astonished by how expensive it was. It didn't take him more than a minute to add everything up once he had them listed. Addition wasn't too bad.

"$48.17."

Cuzzo's eyes bulged. "Dang, that's pricey. So...how do we figure out how much it costs us to make each cup of lemonade?"

Mark's mom brought her hands together in pride. "That's a great question, Danielle."

Cuzzo winced at the sound of her real name. She very much preferred Cuzzo.

"The next step is to find out how many cups of lemonade we actually made."

Mark's mom stood up and grabbed one of the large jugs of finished lemonade and brought it over to the kitchen table. She set it down with a loud clunk.

Mark's heart sunk as the liquid sloshed around inside. "Careful with my acorns," he thought.

"Each of these jugs holds one hundred twenty-eight ounces of liquid, and you got four of 'em. Mark, if you multiply those together, we'll know how many ounces of lemonade we made in total."

Multiplication was starting to push the limits of Mark's confidence, but he continued.

128 x 4

Mark could feel his hands start to sweat. He walked through the steps that Ms. Langston had taught him at least two million five hundred times. "First, do eight times four, carry the two—Why is my heart beating so fast? Focus, focus—four times two is eight. Do I add the two I carried over or multiply it? Oh man, is Cuzzo looking at me? How much time has passed since I started this..." Mark's mind ran wild. He took a deep breath to calm himself down.

Finally, "Five hundred twelve?"

Mark was relieved when he looked up to his mother's smile.

"Ay, good job cousin!"

Mark met Cuzzo's high five midair. Their hands collided so hard that his vibrated for a couple minutes after.

"You're not done, baby. Now each cup you pour should be eight ounces. I marked on this cup with marker what eight ounces looks like so you can get used to pouring that amount as you sell the drinks."

Mark turned the red solo cup around in his hands until he came to the black marker. That' a nice size cup of lemonade. His customers would be pleased.

"Now if each cup has eight ounces, how many cups of lemonade can we get out of these four jugs that total five hundred twelve ounces altogether?"

Without hesitation, Cuzzo grabbed the pen from Mark. He wasn't sure if she was saving him from doing division—something he would appreciate—or taking advantage of the opportunity to show off. Either way, it saved Mark from another mini panic attack. Mark watched Cuzzo write the problem down. Her handwriting was way better than his.

512÷8

Not even 10 seconds passed before Cuzzo shouted out the answer. "Sixty-four!"

Mark wanted to kick her as hard as he could under the table, but what would that accomplish at this point?

"Correct! You've always been so bright." Mark's mom took a seat at the table across from him and Cuzzo.

The scene reminded Mark of a crime movie where the cop tried to get answers out of his suspects in some cold, concrete interrogation room.

"If you sell all of your lemonade, you'll sell approximately sixty-four cups. Now you divide the cost of the ingredients, or $48.17, by the number of possible cups to determine how much it cost us to make each cup. From there, we determine how much to charge for each cup, so we can make a profit!"

His mother's elegant handwriting wrote out the problem as she spoke it.

64÷$48.17= .75

"It cost us about 75 cents to make each glass of that lemonade. Now we know we need to charge more than that in order to make money!"

Mark grabbed the sheet of paper and went over the math four more times to make sure he got it. It made him feel better when Cuzzo had to do the same. It took him a couple minutes, but he understood it. But how much was too much to charge for his lemonade? He had to think. He knew how hard he worked on thinking about this, planning everything, and then finally making it. Eight ounces was a good size cup, and it would be even more valuable because tomorrow was supposed to be one of the hottest days of the year.

Mark looked at Cuzzo. "What do you think... partner?"

Cuzzo tilted her head as she pondered his question. "If we charge $2 and sell ALL sixty-four glasses of lemonade, then we would make $128. But we have to subtract our costs, right?"

Mark's mom nodded but looked at Mark to do the math. She thought this was great practice for him, and Mark didn't disagree.

"What's the profit you make after you subtract your costs, Mark?" Once again, she slid the paper and pencil across the table to him.

$128 − $48.17 = $79.80

Mark's gaze met his mother's just in time to catch the twinkle in her eye. He smiled. "I think that's a great start to a new beginning, huh, Mom?"

9

The Big Day

Cuzzo opened the back door to Uncle Craig's candy red convertible and carefully loaded the lemonade on to the seat. Luckily, the table and signs fit neatly into the trunk, otherwise there was no way Mark and Cuzzo were fitting into the back of the vehicle. Mark buckled his seat belt out of habit, but Cuzzo didn't even bother. Thank goodness the park wasn't more than three miles away because Mark felt like the car was getting smaller by the second. Uncle Craig turned on the ignition and cranked up the volume, blasting music from a time before Mark was born. Cuzzo and Mark snickered as Uncle Craig and Mark's mother sang obnoxiously in the front seat, no care in the world.

"This that ol' head music, boy. You don't know nothing about this!" Uncle Craig was right, but what Mark did know is that he wanted this feeling to last forever.

As Cuzzo and Uncle Craig set up the table that would become the lemonade stand, Mark cautiously took the sign Cuzzo had made the night before out of the trunk. The glue had dried just in time, making the sign shine bright with glitter whenever the light hit it. Cuzzo had done a good job.

They decided on a location right by the playground entrance, which was also fifty feet away from a long stretch of trail where people often rollerbladed and ran.

It was hot. The sweat formed freely on Mark's brow, and within fifteen minutes, Cuzzo's blue shirt already had sweat marks around her armpits. Mark was glad he put on deodorant.

As time passed, everyone started to second-guess the original plan. They had been out there for over an hour and had sold only three glasses, a far shot from the sixty-four they had made.

There were people everywhere, but nobody stopped to give them the time of day. Mark wore his emotions on his sleeve. He was starting to taste the bitterness of failure.

Cuzzo came up behind him and gently grabbed his shoulder. She handed Mark a water bottle. "Mark, we can't give up now!" It was like she could read his mind.

Without saying anything, Mark decided to take a walk. He didn't want to hear her pep talk. Mark walked over to the playground and found a lone swing set away from the main playground and, better yet, away from his family and the lemonade stand. He sat down hard, making the old swing creak. His body was heavy with heat and frustration.

Why weren't people buying his lemonade?! They had worked tirelessly to make it perfect. They could have used the powder stuff, but no, they chose to make it fresh with honey, ginger, and real fruit, leaving it in the freezer so it would be nice and icy by the time they got set up today. He had done everything right, he thought. Mark swung back and forth, the breeze created by the momentum of his body calming him only slightly. He looked up at the sky and closed his eyes. Back and forth he swung like a pendulum.

"You do know that it's not safe to swing with your eyes closed."

Mark opened his eyes but didn't look in the direction of Mansa. He didn't want him to see him cry.

"Feeling bad for yourself doesn't solve one thing."

When Mark looked where he assumed the squirrel would be standing, he saw nothing but an extraordinarily large acorn. Mark raised an eyebrow. "Where are you going with—"

THUMP!

Mansa scurried down the chain of the swing set and jumped down onto Mark's shoulder. Mark was so caught off guard, he stood up. Mansa held tightly onto his ear and steered his head to look down at the massive acorn.

"Remember why you are here." Even though Mansa's voice was stern, demanding obedience, his tone still put him at ease.

Mark's shoulders relaxed, and the large gasp of air he had been holding in came out his nose.

"When we talked about acorns, we also talked about doing things that you love. The reason we choose things we love is so that when our journey gets difficult, we don't give up."

Mark said nothing, but when Mansa tugged on his ear to check if he understood, he nodded in agreement.

"The acorns I gather in summer and autumn to prepare for winter when there are no acorns do not appear in front of my home like a package from Amazon, Mark."

Mark had never considered this, but it made sense. Mansa would have to gather food to eat now, but also for months when the acorns no longer fell from the trees. If he didn't, he would STARVE.

"You need to want this like I want my acorns. The reward of success is not going to happen without work." Mansa paused, paw still gripped on Mark's earlobe, holding him to attention like he was some kind of soldier.

Mark waited on his every word.

"Have you told the people walking by on the trail that you have cold lemonade? No, you have not! Have you approached the children taking breaks from their game of tag that you have something that will give them a boost of energy for the next game? The parents who sit in the shade of the big oak, do you ask if they would like a light refreshment while they watch their children and catch up with their friends?"

Mark had assumed the sign and stand would tell everyone all they needed to know. He had never thought to SELL the lemonade. When Mark went to the corner store with Cuzzo to get candy, no one SOLD him the candy, but that's because they came there in search of candy. People didn't come to the park for lemonade. They came to play. It was his job to convince them they needed his lemonade to make their time there even BETTER.

Mark felt that fire deep in his belly billow up into his chest again. "I'm so glad I met you, Mansa."

Mark started to run as fast as he could back to the table where Cuzzo and Uncle Craig were waiting. They were openly annoyed that Mark had disappeared.

"Where the heck have you been?" asked Cuzzo.

He ignored her question and grabbed her by the shoulders with both hands. "You grab the sign, the beautiful perfect sign that you made and that I am so thankful for, and go stand by the trail with the biggest and best smile you got and wave at every dang person who walks by, OK?!"

Cuzzo looked confused but listened. Something about Mark's sudden determination made her trust that he knew something she didn't.

And he did.

Uncle Craig looked curiously at Mark. He didn't stop him, instead he listened as Mark told him to man the stand and handle the money. Uncle Craig, not used to taking orders from eleven-year-olds, smiled and gave Mark a salute. "Sir, yes, sir."

Mark saluted back before jogging over to the big oak that sat at the front of the playground. Underneath its outstretched branches sat two long blue benches where moms, dads, and nannies sat shielded from the sun. Some women had made fans out of loose papers from their purses, while several of the men had white rags draped over their heads to collect the beads of salty water that dripped from their brows.

Mark stopped just before the oldest gentleman and cleared his throat, hoping his voice didn't shake as it carried the words he would say next. "Afternoon, ladies and gentlemen, is everyone here as hot as I am?"

One of the women let out a long and exaggerated "hmmmmmm hmmmmmm."

One of the older men, skeptical of Mark's intentions, said, "And what are you gonna do about it, young man?"

"Despite his heart pounding out of his chest and his entire body wanting to turn and run back to the swing set where Mansa had been, Mark smiled. "I'm glad you asked sir. My mother, cousin, and I stayed up half the night making lemonade from my grandmother's old southern recipe. It contains all fresh ingredients, and to prepare for today's heat, we put it in the freezer until we came here this afternoon so it would be nice and icy for your enjoyment. As someone whose favorite drink has been lemonade for my entire life, I highly recommend it. It's $2 for a full glass, and I would love to get each of you one."

Mark made himself look the older man in the eyes before he finished speaking. Well, he looked at his nose, but same thing, right? The man's face was expressionless, as if he didn't hear a single word Mark said. Then, out of nowhere, he let out a loud billowing laugh that seemed to be contagious as everyone else around Mark joined in.

Mark laughed nervously. Running away seemed like the best solution at this point, and just as he was starting to turn away, the man reached for his arm.

"I'll take four, one for me, my lady over there, and my two boys who are about two monkey bars away from passing out." He grabbed his wallet from his back pocket and turned to the man sitting next to him. "Marty, you want one?"

The man looked at Mark and shook his head. "Not interested, kid."

Mark thought rejection would hurt more, but he didn't even care. He was high off the sale he didn't think he would get. He collected the man's $8 and turned to the rest of the bench. "Anyone else?"

An awkward pause followed. It probably lasted for two seconds, but it felt like minutes. Mark couldn't hear kids screaming, no metal clanking from the jungle gym, no laughter... until FINALLY, two people raised their hands.

Then three!

Mark felt like there was electricity pulsing through his veins. He wasn't even hot anymore. As he jogged back to the lemonade stand, he stopped to take in the view before him.

There was a LINE of people. Uncle Craig was busy collecting money and didn't notice Mark until he slammed the money down next to him. "Boy, what in the..."

"That's $14, Uncle Craig."

Uncle Craig looked down at the change and then back up at Mark. "Now, I don't know what came up and bit you when you ran away for ten minutes, but you go on and tell that snake or bug to come on and bite my butt too, 'cus you're making some change here, boy!"

Mark opened the cooler where they kept the jugs of lemonade to start working on the large order for the blue bench brigade, who turned out to be his best customers so far. They had just a little more than two jugs left.

On Mark's way back from delivering the drinks to the blue benches, he saw his life flash before his eyes as a ball whizzed by his face.

"Head's up!"

"Aren't you supposed to say that BEFORE the ball almost kills someone?" Mark thought. Mark turned around angrily to face the kid whose terrible aim nearly knocked him out.

"Mark! What's up, dude?" It was Jimmy.

"Oh, hey, man…"

"My bad, dude, that was a terrible throw. What are you doing here?"

Six more boys ran up behind Jimmy. Mark recognized them all from school as Jimmy's posse.

"Everything cool over here, Jimmy?" One of the boys said.

Mark couldn't tell which one, but it didn't matter. All of Jimmy's minions were pretty much clones of each other. Tall, perfect haircuts, shoes that Mark's mom would never buy for him, clothes that would be considered Mark's Sunday best.

Jimmy didn't acknowledge the boy. He waited patiently with a polite smile on his face for Mark to answer. Mark wanted to dislike Jimmy so bad, but he couldn't. He really was a nice guy.

Mark cleared his throat. "My grandmother has this secret recipe for her icy lemonade, and my mom and cousin and I made a batch of it and are selling it at the front of the playground. It's delicious, and because it's so hot, it's selling like hotcakes."

Immediately, Jimmy's face lit up with excitement. "Bro, that's awesome! I LOVE lemonade. How much for a glass?"

A couple of Jimmy's minions spoke out in agreement, "Yea, me too."

"Man, that sounds good right about now."

Mark looked down at Jimmy as he dug around in his pockets and pulled out a crisp twenty-dollar bill. "My dad gave me $20 in case I wanted to get something while I was out. Can I get as much as this will buy me?"

There was only one customer at the stand when Mark got back, but as he got closer, he saw the person delicately balancing four red cups as he walked back to his family. Uncle Craig, with his hands on his hips, nodded in satisfaction. By the time Mark poured the ten cups for Jimmy and his boys (he felt bad for calling them minions now that they had bought so much lemonade), there was only one jug left.

Cuzzo returned from her post on the trail. "Man, y'all, I need a break."

Mark was tired too, but they were so close to selling out. They had to give it their all. "Who haven't we sold to?" he asked Uncle Craig and Cuzzo.

Neither of them answered, but the old man from the oak tree did. "Just about everybody in this dang park."

Mark turned around in shock. Uh oh, had he forgotten someone's order? Did he give him the wrong change? Mark scanned his brain for errors.

"How much you got left, youngin?"

Mark looked down at the lonely jug lying in the cooler.

"We're almost out. We got about sixteen cups left."

"And how much might that be?" the man asked.

Mark froze as he frantically tried to do the multiplication in his head.

16 cups x $2

Six times two is twelve, carry the one, two times one is two, two plus one is three... "THIRTY TWO!" Mark said too loudly.

The older man looked at Mark with the same expressionless face he offered up an hour earlier, except this time, Mark was ready for the deep, hearty laugh that followed. "You got yourself a deal, young blood," he said between chuckles. He threw a twenty, a ten, and a five-dollar bill on the counter. "Keep the change. It's nice to see young men and women like yourself out here learning something that matters. Keep it up. You're going places in life." He grabbed the jug and ten clean red cups and headed back to his family and friends.

Cuzzo collapsed into Uncle Craig's lawn chair, tilted her head back, and closed her eyes. Mark sat on the ground across from her. He closed his eyes and told his brain to remember this for as long as he lived.

With his eyes closed, Mark could appreciate what was happening around him in greater detail. The grass tickled his wrists and legs. The smell of the sweet lemonade mixed with the scent of sunscreen was so strong he could almost taste it. There were birds chirping and laughter coming in waves from every direction. A cool breeze kissed his cheeks, sending a shiver down his spine.

This is awesome, he thought.

Uncle Craig opened up a smaller cooler that he was keeping inside the car. One that Mark didn't notice he had. He pulled out three ice-cold water bottles filled with the lemonade they had just finished selling out of. Uncle Craig handed one to Cuzzo and the other to Mark.

Mark guzzled half of the bottle without taking a breath. The sticky nectar dripped down his face and neck, leaving a fresh puddle on his already damp shirt.

Uncle Craig sat down next to Mark and draped his heavy arm over his shoulders. He leaned in close and spoke to Mark in a way he was not accustomed to. "You know, you're the closest thing I've got to a son and... well, at least I like to think... that I'm the closest thing you got to a dad... I want you to know, Mark, that what you did today wasn't much different than what I do every day. You got what it takes to be better than I ever will be. Remember that, son."

"Son," Mark repeated in his head.

Uncle Craig gave Mark a hard slam on the back, nearly knocking the wind out of him. "And don't worry about the water bottles. I put an extra $20 in the money bag before I filled them up for y'all. What kind of man would I be if I didn't support our local businesses?"

Mark didn't know if it was the heat or the gravity of the last several minutes of conversation, but he couldn't fight the urge to laugh. It bubbled up and out of his mouth uncontrollably, sending happiness from his feet to his face. He wasn't worried about Uncle Craig not paying for the lemonade. He wasn't even worried about counting the money they just made. For the first time, the boy who was always worried about his future wasn't so worried at all.

THE END

Made in the USA
Middletown, DE
11 October 2023

40652721R00040